BOOK ANALYSIS

Bright
≡Summaries.com

Rameau's Nephew

BY DENIS DIDEROT

BOOK ANALYSIS

Written by Juline Hombourger
Translated by Emma Hanna

Rameau's Nephew

BY DENIS DIDEROT

Bright
≡Summaries.com

Shed new light
on your favorite books with

Bright
≡Summaries.com

www.brightsummaries.com

DENIS DIDEROT

FRENCH WRITER, PHILOSOPHER AND ENCYCLOPAEDIA EDITOR

- **Born in Langres (France) in 1713.**
- **Died in Paris in 1784.**
- **Notable works:**
  - *D'Alembert's Dream*, (1782) philosophical tale
  - *Jacques the Fatalist* (1796), novel
  - *Paradox of the Actor* (1830), essay

Denis Diderot was a novelist, playwright, art critic and one of the most illustrious thinkers of the Age of Enlightenment in the 18th century. He was a passionate believer in freedom, and spent four months in Vincennes prison because of his outspokenness. From 1746 onwards, Diderot and the French mathematician and philosopher Jean le Rond d'Alembert (1717-1783) began working on the *Encyclopédie*, an ambitious project that aimed to compile the entirety of human knowledge. In spite of the challenges they faced because of censorship, the *Encyclopédie* is considered one of the greatest successes of the Enlightenment. As well as this monumental work, Diderot wrote a number of other texts, and garnered recognition for his writings on theatre and aesthetics, his reflections on morality and his many philosophical dialogues.

RAMEAU'S NEPHEW

THE PHILOSOPHICAL QUESTIONS OF THE 18TH CENTURY

- **Genre:** satirical novel
- **Reference edition:** Diderot, D. (2001) *Rameau's Nephew*. Trans. Barzun, J. and Bowen, R. H. Indianapolis/Cambridge: Hackett.
- **1st edition:** 1891
- **Themes:** philosophy, morality, education, happiness, flattery, music

Rameau's Nephew, or the Second Satire was written between 1761 or 1762 and 1780. The novel takes the form of a philosophical dialogue between a philosopher and the nephew of the French composer Jean-Philippe Rameau (1683-1764). The two men begin a conversation which seems to frequently digress from the main subject, but which is lively and stimulating nevertheless. This conversation is centred on the topic of morality, and it soon becomes clear that the two characters have extremely different views on this subject: while the philosopher asserts that virtuous behaviour allows people to lead happy lives, Rameau's nephew is convinced that the only way to make the most of life is to listen to reason, even if this leads to immorality. The novel's main purpose is to question and challenge firmly-held beliefs on both sides, meaning that the argument is inconclusive, with neither character emerging as a clear winner.

SUMMARY

Rameau's Nephew is not divided into parts or chapters; instead, each theme addressed in the text is set apart from the others by means of interludes between them, during which the nephew often sings or plays some kind of musical instrument. This summary follows the same thematic structure as the novel.

INTRODUCTION

The narrator, who is a philosopher and is given no name other than "MYSELF", often goes to the Regency Café near Port-Royal in Paris to watch the other customers play chess. One day, he meets Rameau's nephew ("HE") there. The narrator describes him as an inherently contradictory individual who is equally comfortable with elegant speech and vulgarity, and who can look emaciated one day but plump and healthy the next – in other words, he is a chameleon whose nature is ever-shifting. The nephew greets the philosopher: "Ha ha! So there you are, master Philosopher! And what are you up to among all these idlers? Do you waste your time too, pushing wood?" (pp. 10-11). With that, their debate begins.

THEME 1: GENIUS

The philosopher briefly asks the nephew about his relationship with his uncle, who is a famous composer. HE admits that he is jealous of his uncle's genius, especially because geniuses never think about anyone but themselves and tend to be emotionally distant from their families. HE's description of genius makes it seem like an inherently negative trait which can have dangerous consequences for society as a whole, despite also being the driving force behind its advancement. MYSELF counters this argument by saying that there have been geniuses who were good men, such as Socrates (Greek philosopher, 5th century BCE), and that even though geniuses may act in ways that are harmful to a few individuals, this pain is outweighed by the happiness that a genius's work can bring to future generations, citing Jean Racine (French playwright, 1639-1699) as proof. However, this does not answer the original question of how geniuses can be judged, and HE eventually admits that in spite of every-thing, he would give anything to be a genius.

THEME 2: SOCIAL SCROUNGING

The nephew imitates his uncle by singing some of his music, after which the two men pick up their conversation again. The nephew describes himself as "an ignoramus, a fool, a lunatic, a lazy, impudent, greedy good-for-nothing (p. 18), and says that he has been thrown out of the house he was staying in because he said something that his host judged too reasonable. MYSELF advises him to go back to them as soon as possible because even though the nephew believes that he is irreplaceable, this may not be the case. HE dismisses this suggestion by saying that he still has his dignity and that he will not go and beg for them to take him back under any circumstances; his only regret is that he did not spend more time leeching off the wealthy and putting the tricks he learned on the streets to use to amass a fortune of his own. MYSELF is horrified by this mindset, which he deems appallingly callous.

THEME 3: EDUCATION

The nephew performs once again, showing off his musical talents for the philosopher's benefit. He then discusses teaching methods, and asserts that children should be taught singing, dancing and music. The philosopher disagrees, and claims that grammar, history and ethics are much more important. At this point, their friendly discussion turns heated, and HE eventually declares that his approach to teaching was no worse than any other, because he was aware of his own lack of knowledge and therefore spent his time gossiping instead of actually teaching his pupils anything. This meant that he could be sure that he had not passed any of his own mistakes on to them, and that they would therefore have nothing to unlearn when they moved on to a more qualified teacher.

THEME 4: MORALITY

HE argues that moral principles are flexible and depend on the circumstances at hand, but that money is always the most important factor because it makes anything possible. HE also believes that it is perfectly acceptable to take advantage of the rich, and claims that if he were to become rich himself he would abuse his position the same way all wealthy people do.

THEME 5: HAPPINESS

HE begins mocking MYSELF and his moral principles, as he does not believe that happiness can be found through patriotism, social standing or being considerate towards one's friends and family. The philosopher tries to change his mind by using examples that show how his own happiness motivates him to aid those in need. Indeed, MYSELF believes that honesty and happiness are inextricably linked, although the nephew points out that it is difficult to be happy when you are dying of hunger, and that the effort the virtuous put into repressing their vices drains their lives of all happiness. He notes that he would never count himself among their number, as he freely indulges in the pleasures of the senses and fully embraces his free will and lack of hypocrisy.

THEME 6: THE ART OF FLATTERY

The nephew discusses the skill of flattery, which is one of his specialties. He briefly describes a few of the patrons who have employed him over the years, explaining how their deep misery made it very difficult to entertain them, particularly as there was very little they wanted other than to be flattered. Luckily for him, he has mastered the art of flattery, and knows exactly how to use the right pretences, tone of voice and gestures to get into the good graces of the wealthy.

THEME 7: LITERATURE

The philosopher brings the conversation back to the nephew's life with his former employers, the Bertins, and HE goes through a list of all the people who were invited to dine with them. HE also takes this chance to mock several of them, particularly with regard to their supposed erudition. This brings them to the topic of literature, and HE claims that he uses books as a source of inspiration for his habit of playing the fool, as they often contain attitudes that he can mimic. Once again, HE returns to the topic of the right way to deal with rich people, and mentions that he was content during his time with the Bertins because people used to seek out his company, knowing that he had a reputation for being amusing. This leads him to ask what true vulgarity is.

THEME 8: THE SUBLIME

The conversation suddenly shifts dramatically in tone, as HE asserts that a master criminal garners much more admiration than a petty thief, backing this claim up with the example of a renegade from Avignon who conned a Jew out of a large sum of money and then handed him over to the Inquisition. HE argues that the renegade's actions are so awful that they become sublime, which is such a bold claim that it makes the philosopher feel nauseous.

THEME 9: MUSIC

The nephew sings a victory song, after which the two characters discuss singing. HE states that he finds the work of up-and-coming young musicians to be very powerful and honest, sparking a long digression about music, which they analyse in great detail. The nephew then performs yet again, this time pouring his heart and soul into the songs and single-handedly making an entire opera come to life in the café. This leads to a discussion about the art of playing music, and the nephew makes his preference for Italian music over French music – and, by extension, over his uncle's music – abundantly clear. In a way, this section of the novel revives the old quarrel between the Ancients and the Moderns (an artistic and literary debate that divided the leading figures of the cultural landscape of 17th-century France).

THEME 10: NATURE VERSUS NURTURE

MYSELF ponders the way the nephew manages to combine such incredible elegance with such a lack of moral decency, and HE replies that it is doubtlessly a matter of heredity. He believes that if a person's heredity (meaning their nature) is corrupt, their upbringing is unlikely to improve matters much; at most, a virtuous upbringing will shape them into an average person who is neither exceptionally virtuous nor exceptionally prone to vice. The nephew also says that he is most anxious to teach his son about the value and importance of money, as it is only possible to get everything you want – or, at the very least, to laugh at everything – when you have money. The philosopher admits that the nephew is starting to frustrate him, but he is also forced to acknowledge that HE has one major virtue: an utter lack of hypocrisy.

THEME 11: THE NEPHEW'S FAILURE

HE admits that he has great admiration for MYSELF's knowledge. In fact, he wishes that he were equally knowledgeable, as this would enable him to lie more easily and make his fortune. The philosopher claims that money does not matter to him, and he then asks the nephew why he has never put his talents as a musician to work. HE admits that he is stupid and that he has been spoiled by his pleasure-seeking and by the fact that society does not encourage people to do great deeds. No matter how hard he has tried, he has never been successful. The philosopher reminds him that mime is a universal language, and the nephew responds by mimicking various people. According to MYSELF, who cites the example of Diogenes and the Cynics, it is only possible to live a life without pretences by becoming a philosopher. However, the nephew ignores this advice, and says that he has no intention of changing his behaviour. He only has one regret: namely, losing his wife, who could have made him rich. At that moment, the clock chimes and the two men leave, and the book ends as Rameau's nephew says: "He laughs best who laughs last" (p. 87).

CHARACTER STUDY

In *Rameau's Nephew*, Diderot creates a dialogue between two characters whose worldviews seem to be diametrically opposed, but which could also be seen as two sides of the same coin.

THE NEPHEW (HE)

We are not given much information about HE, although we do learn that he was married, has lost his wife and has a child. He is also the nephew of a famous composer from Diderot's time, which is made clear in the novel by the time he spends singing, performing and talking about music. However, he also rebels against his heritage, and prefers Italian music to his uncle's work.

HE describes himself as a social parasite who leeches off his patrons and who places more value on pleasure-seeking than on adhering to any kind of moral principles. He has no qualms about playing the fool in order to achieve his goals, which often involve entertaining the rich and powerful to make a living. This well-spoken idiot freely admits to being contradictory by nature, even when he knows that it will earn him the disapproval of others, and this trait fascinates the philosopher, as does his utter lack of hypocrisy. In fact, HE criticises philosophers, saying that their dogma is hypocritical because it is impossible to put it into practice in everyday life.

HE strongly believes that happiness can only be found through amorality, and defends this belief using the reason why he was dismissed from his position with his former employers, the Bertins, as an example. They threw him out because when a visiting abbé was seated at the head of the table during a dinner, HE told him that he would not necessarily be given such a prestigious seat again in the future. Because of this remark, which he considers to be perfectly reasonable and full of common sense (though clearly uttered at the wrong time and in front of the wrong people), he was doomed to sink back into poverty, even though his presence at the house had previously been celebrated.

The character of HE can be linked to the literary archetype of the fool, which dates back to medieval times, as one of his defining characteristics is his ability to distance himself from society in order to mock it. Indeed, HE represents everything that is disdained by society, and embodies this role so perfectly that others seem to almost admire him for it. However, he is also a complex individual, and glimpses of a more virtuous side to his nature occasionally peek through. Furthermore, he can also be considered an early example of the literary archetype of the eccentric genius.

THE PHILOSOPHER (MYSELF)

The narrator's defining characteristic is his role as a philosopher, and therefore as a thinker. At the start of the novel, he notes that he habitually debates a variety of subjects with himself, showing that he is the embodiment of rational thought. He is inquisitive by nature and very well-educated, and he lives with his wife and 8-year-old daughter. In his opinion, happiness can only be found through virtue, and he firmly believes in the importance of values such as charity, respect, friendship and justice.

The philosopher genuinely admires the nephew, in spite of his disturbingly amoral tendencies.

He seems charmed by the nephew's frenetic energy, laughs at his antics and is delighted by his musical performances. However, this kinship is not quite enough to negate their differences of opinion, and the nephew leaves the philosopher feeling thoroughly wrong-footed. In fact, one of the questions that appears most frequently throughout the novel is: "How is it that with such fineness of feeling, so much sensibility where musical beauty is concerned, you are blind to the beauties of morality, so insensible to the charm of virtue?" (p. 71).

Even so, upon closer inspection it becomes apparent that the two men are not as different as they seem. Although the philosopher holds his moral principles dear, he also acknowledges the value of sensuality, as he believes that nature and the senses have an undeniable effect on our daily life and way of thinking, and the role they play in our lives is therefore impossible to dismiss out of hand. As such, the two men's beliefs on the subject of pleasure are relatively well-aligned.

These two characters could be interpreted as two sides of the author's own personality, with MYSELF representing Diderot's philosophical, reasonable side, and HE representing his eccentric, libertine side. This interpretation also allows the novel to be viewed as a dramatization of Diderot's own internal monologue.

ANALYSIS

FROM *SATURA* TO SATIRE

Rameau's Nephew is subtitled the *Second Satire*, which makes it clear that the text should be classified as a satirical work. This genre takes its name from *satura*, a term that was used during antiquity to denote a collection of poetry which contained a wide variety of works from the genres of comedy, tragedy and everything in between.

Accordingly, satirical works generally combine the traits of multiple other literary genres. Furthermore, *Rameau's Nephew* features a number of characteristics which are more commonly associated with theatrical works (such as everything each character says being preceded by their name, which is capitalised), and the inclusion of a narrator is reminiscent of a tale.

Furthermore, the novel does not have a rigid structure, and each theme discussed by the two protagonists flows smoothly into the next without any kind of organisational distinction between them, aside from the occasional musical interludes. This makes the dialogue seem more like a spontaneous exchange, thereby giving it a more realistic feel which is heightened by the fact that neither of the characters emerges as the winner of the argument.

The term "satire" also evokes the concept of using humour as a vehicle for criticism. One of Diderot's motivations for writing *Rameau's Nephew* was to respond to one of his detractors, Charles Palissot de Montenoy (French playwright, 1730-1814), who had fiercely criticised the philosopher in one of his plays in 1761. In a move that was rather typical of the 18th century, particularly with regard to the squabbles that plagued the publication of the *Encyclopédie*, Diderot used a literary work of his own (namely, *Rameau's Nephew*) as the framework for his rebuttal. However, he also used the novel to criticise society's moral failings, the unequal distribution of wealth and the ways the most powerful members of society abused their position, as well as to challenge the prevailing aesthetic fashions.

MATERIALISM

According to modern philosophical conventions, Diderot's worldview can be classified as materialist, as is made clear by the dialogue in *Rameau's Nephew*. Materialism is a branch of philosophy which holds that everything that exists, including human beings, is composed of matter and moving particles. This stands in contrast to both dualist philosophy and Christian doctrine, which teaches that the soul is immaterial.

HE and MYSELF both subscribe to a materialist outlook, though in different ways. The nephew does not believe in any higher moral authority, and instead believes that nothing is more important than seeking sensual pleasure, since nothing is permanent or immutable and all human beings meet the same end: "To rot under marble or to rot in bare earth is still to rot" (p. 24). Meanwhile, the philosopher's brand of materialism is more moral in nature, as he believes that familiarity with a higher moral authority comes through experience. For example, he recognises that money is important, but advocates using it in a virtuous manner.

IRONY AND OPEN DIALOGUE

Dialogue was an extremely fashionable literary genre during the 18th century. A dialogue consists of a transcription of a real or fictional conversation during which a number of ideas are debated. There were several reasons why this genre was so popular among the philosophers of the Enlightenment:

- it is instructive in nature, as it introduces the reader to a number of philosophical standpoints;
- the inclusion of multiple characters allows the author to explore a variety of different points of view and express a certain degree of uncertainty and hesitation by leaving the discussion open-ended;
- it allows encourages the reader to ask questions of their own, thus allowing them to hone their critical thinking skills.

Indeed, in *Rameau's Nephew*, Diderot addresses a number of different points of view, thus encouraging the reader to re-evaluate their own opinions.

The novel also features several different forms of irony, including the nephew's cynicism and the philosopher's antiphrasis. Both protagonists challenge the other and try to leave them off-kilter: MYSELF is more intent on trying to understand HE and sway him to his own way of thinking, whereas HE seems to simply enjoy provoking MYSELF, though he also attempts to make him doubt his beliefs. In some ways, the nephew could be seen as the devil on the philosopher's shoulder, making him an active participant in the Socratic method of revealing the truth.

In any case, both protagonists play a key role in the discussion, and the exploration of both sides of this argument remains the novel's main goal.

FURTHER REFLECTION

- Besides the fact that he overtly describes himself as a fool, why else can the nephew be associated with this literary archetype?
- What role does music play in *Rameau's Nephew*?
- How is the text structured? In your opinion, what is the underlying logic behind the way it is organised?
- What role do each of the two protagonists play in the novel?
- In your opinion, could this dialogue be rewritten as a monologue?
- In your opinion, which character wins the argument?
- To what extent could Diderot's writing style be described as lively and natural?
- Discuss the metaphors used in the text.
- In your opinion, why did Diderot refrain from publishing this novel during his lifetime? Do

you think he was afraid it would be censored?

- To what extent is *Rameau's Nephew* reminiscent of the *Encyclopédie*?
- What similarities exist between *Rameau's Nephew* and other works by Diderot such as *Jacques the Fatalist* and *D'Alembert's Dream*?

We want to hear from you!
Leave a comment on your online library
and share your favourite books on social media!

FURTHER READING

REFERENCE EDITION

- Diderot, D. (2001) *Rameau's Nephew*. Trans. Barzun, J. and Bowen, R. H. Indianapolis/ Cambridge: Hackett.

REFERENCE STUDIES

- Delon, M. (2004) Preface to *Le Neveu de Rameau*. Paris: Gallimard.

- Fontenay, É. (2001) *Diderot ou le Matérialisme enchanté*. Paris: Grasset.

- Jauss, H. R. (1984) *The Dialogical and the Dialectical Neveu de Rameau*. Center for Hermeneutical Studies.

MORE FROM BRIGHTSUMMARIES.COM

- Reading guide – *Jacques the Fatalist* by Denis Diderot.

- Reading guide – *The Nun* by Denis Diderot.

BOOK ANALYSIS

Bright ≡Summaries.com

More guides to rediscover your love of literature

Animal Farm
BY GEORGE ORWELL

The Stranger
BY ALBERT CAMUS

Harry Potter and the Sorcerer's Stone
BY J.K. ROWLING

The Silence of the Sea
BY VERCORS

Antigone
BY JEAN ANOUILH

The Flowers of Evil
BY BAUDELAIRE

www.brightsummaries.com

Although the editor makes every effort to
verify the accuracy of the information published,
BrightSummaries.com accepts no responsibility for
the content of this book.

© BrightSummaries.com, 2018. All rights reserved.

www.brightsummaries.com

Ebook EAN: 9782808010856

Paperback EAN: 9782808010863

Legal Deposit: D/2018/12603/282

Cover: © Primento

Digital conception by Primento, the digital partner of
publishers.